BETRAYAL

Break the Cyclic Pain of Betrayal

In Five Steps

ANA LEEN

In service of Our Lord Jesus Christ

Betrayal

Break the Cyclic Pain of Betrayal
(In Five Steps)

Author: Ana Leen
Cover Design: Reychelle Ann Ignacio
Photo: Viktor Hancek
Proof Reading: Albert Bright
Editing: Hazlo Emma

First Edition, 2018. Ana Leen (Ana Leen Jo Centre)
Book 1 in the Book Series Betrayal

ISBN 978-1-7901-0723-0

Kindle Version: ASIN: B07KTJN7SY

Printed and Bound in the United States of America

First Printing December 2018

For special *discounts for bulk purchases, sales promotions, and educational needs, contact sales(at)analeenie.com or fill in your name and contact details here goo.gl/forms/zQciH5xs3uNQUHsa2*

Unless otherwise stated, bible verses are taken from the Amplified Bible, Classic Edition (AMPC)

Connect on Twitter (at)LeenGoto for a free counselling session on the first 30 minutes and join the Pinterest tribe at pinterest.com/AnaLeenie/.

Ana Leen Jo Centre
analeenie.com

Disclaimer

The advice and strategies found within may not be suitable for every situation. Reading this book does not substitute for advice of a competent therapist or certified counselor authorized to work in your jurisdiction. Every effort has been made to ensure that the content provided is accurate and helpful for our readers at publishing time.

However, this is not exhaustive treatment of the subjects. The advice and strategies found within may not be suitable for every situation. The view points are those of Ana Leen in addition to experiences over the past twenty plus years while counseling. The intention of this book is to share her life's successes and struggles with the subject matter therein, and what has worked.

All attempts have been made to verify the information provided by this book. Neither the author nor the publisher assumes any responsibility for errors, omission, or contrary interpretation of anything written herein.

The views expressed are those of the author should not be taken as commands. The reader is responsible for his or her future actions, own choices, and results. Notwithstanding, it is possible that by taking into action the steps listed in this book the odds of living in healthy relationships free from the pain, stigma, guilt, and pain of betrayal in the future is of a much higher probability.

The views expressed are based on her personal experiences within ministry, corporate world, education, and everyday life. This work is sold with the understanding that neither the author nor the publisher are held responsible for any assumed losses or damages, in addition to the results accrued from the advice in this publication or information provided herein.

Dedication

To every broken heart.

14 I will confess and praise You for You are fearful and wonderful and for the awful wonder of my birth! Wonderful are Your works, and that my inner self knows right well.

15 My frame was not hidden from You when I was being formed in secret [and] intricately and curiously wrought [as if embroidered with various colors] in the depths of the earth [a region of darkness and mystery].

16 Your eyes saw my unformed substance, and in Your book all the days [of my life] were written before ever they took shape, when as yet there was none of them.

Psalms 139 (AMPC)

Table of Contents

Preface

Break Free Today from the Bond of Betrayal

Do you live clouded by the pain of betrayal with all manner of associated, stigma, shame, and guilt?

Do you worry that this is how you will live for the rest of your life?

Do you have trouble breaking free and letting go?

Are you trapped in the cyclic bond of betrayal?

Do you fear to lose your partner or caregiver forever?

Are you feeling like you are in a codependent relationship?

I have been there and I know what it is like.

Ashamed

Stigmatized

Embarrassed

Destroyed confidence

Poor productivity

Relationships of poor quality

The inability to enjoy life

Stigma, pain, and guilt of betrayal can be obsessively hopeless – the shame of losing a spouse, a close friend, trusted family member – notwithstanding the sense of never being able to feel happy ever again.

Put an end to this TODAY.

No more fear.

No more guilt.

No more failure.

No more trauma.

You are not naïve.

Start living again.

You think it's tough?

STRUGGLE No more.

This easy to read book reveals to you the steps and power in your hands to shift this today.

Receive the healing from past hurt once and for all.

Here's why?

- In this book, you will learn;

- The key aesthetics of betrayal and a betrayed person (Chapter 2)

- How the step by step plan of breaking free from the cycle of betrayal has rescued relationships (yours included)

toward acceptance (Chapter 5)

- How others have tapped into this process and received their freedom, healing, and peace. You too will receive yours. (Testimonials)

- And because you are my loyal reader, you get to be an early bird in the Dream It, Pen It team to receive the next book before anyone else – even before any publishing house (One last thing)

Dive in and embark on the road to recovery.

Set yourself free from any form of abuse and stigma of betrayal

"Feeling sorry for yourself, and your present condition, is not only a waste of energy but the worst habit you could possibly have."

Dale Carnegie

Introduction

Betrayal and denial is a topic rarely discussed at least prior to the reality of it. No one tells you or ever prepares you for the eventuality of betrayal or denial by a close relative, a spouse, a friend, business partner, an acquaintance or anyone for that matter. There are no lessons or degrees offered to help you cope with betrayal when it comes;

One reason could be it is most likely going to come your way one way or another if it hasn't come already. When you are born into this world you are either faced with immediate challenges at birth or cushioned from the pain - if born to loving parents who are endowed with godly wisdom and material wealth, love and care.

When you cry you are held in love and affection, warm, comfort and all you need is provided for you. While this goes on for a period of time, you find that those that you love soon leave you and go away to work or attend to their daily routine while you wait alone whether asleep or in your waking moments.

You soon learn that you will not always have your loved ones neither your way after all, despite your longings and desires to be close to them. Schedules are made for meal times and when to eat or abstain based on others understanding of what time you ought to eat. Notwithstanding, decisions are made for which meals to each and the choice of the food or drink.

On the contrary, even when you are hungry you will not always be fed as opposed to the feeding on demand that you had earlier enjoyed. This is not only limited to meals but also to time given to bonding love and care which is now meted in doses.

Some will advise caregivers not to hold the babies too much least they get used to it and disturb you when you need to be doing more important things so to speak. They are almost saying that the children may be addicted to your love and care and may become societal misfits. This brings to question the preparedness of the society or individual - for that matter - to deal with the issues of life so that what you don't understand or can't deal with what to condemn or proscribe.

When you don't have a remedy or prescription to issues of life shouldn't you seek to find or understand rather than run away or mutilate or stop or discourage those that try to figure out the answers or remedies to those issues?

Picture this.

You start to pursue a purpose and subsequently you share your thoughts or vision with somebody. Along the journey they may not understand you.

Betrayal

What happens then?

More often than not they dump you along the way. They could also discourage or steal your dreams and make them theirs.

Could you have experienced this?

It is no or small wonder then that we have missions that lack visionaries. This is because only the vision carriers have the full awareness of the vision and only they can deliver the desired result. Destiny snatchers or thieves of dreams may be those that are close to us or not, but they all intend to kill the vision or abort it all together.

Human beings, being social, will often find themselves walking the journey and trusting people they find along the way. This cuts across dimensions of life, be it relational, work or otherwise. We share ourselves in all dimensions of life.

In doing so, we end up exposing ourselves to betrayal. People conditionally love and give of themselves. Information is traded for 'what's there in it for me'.

This will be done consciously or unconsciously depending on the intention of the individuals involved. People will join the winning teams to gain economic gain or boost their self-esteem or worth. Some will enter relationships to fill in their gaps or inadequacies or capacity building in areas they deem less endowed.

This may be healthy in some instances, where we complement one another and strengthen each other for a common goal purpose. Unfortunately, more often than not we find ourselves being used, abused, and dumped once a certain purpose is accomplished by those we once thought were our close friends, relatives, colleagues, and even soul mates.

To what extent then do we draw the line between giving of ourselves and being betrayed in whichever context of life based on our understanding of the discomfort it will cost us as individuals?

For mothers and fathers, it may or will cost us time and resources as well as energy, both physical and emotional, not to mention mental and psychological energies expended in the process of bringing up our children.

On the other hand, our parents are judged by a different measure based on our understanding of them and feel betrayed. We measure out to our children what is convenient for us. Often times, we determine the number of changes of clothes, the size and colour, as well as the frequency of the changes of clothes, probably once a year during Christmas.

Likewise, church assembly, school, career, job or place to live in are determined. To a large extent this includes which spouse to marry, from which race, tribe, clan, academic level social status, height, weight, colours, and all manner of set standards that the minds of parents can conceive. Sadly, we may not choose even the lives we live because it is determined by someone real or imagined that we play out to please.

Like the adolescents we seem to have an imaginary audience all through our lives whom we owe allegiance to, and must work hard to entertain or please or risk losing the clout. We get crazier in our quest to keep our audience well entertained.

Our parents, clients, family members, all come back to us for more. The list is endless on the demands made or expected of us, whether they are real or in our imaginations. Certain standards are set for us by those who have not met their own targets.

Isn't it absurd that bars are raised at will or as the society may deem appropriate?

"And he came up to Jesus at once and said, 'Hail (greetings, good health to You, long life to You), Master'! And he embraced Him and kissed Him with [pretended] warmth and devotion."

Matthew 26:49 (AMPC)

Chapter 1

The Pain of Betrayal

What is betrayal?

Betrayal is the act or fact of violating the trust or confidence of another. There is perhaps no greater sadness or insult to a relationship than betrayal. It robs us of a sense of security and belief that we had in another.

Betrayal is a sense of being harmed by the intentional actions, or omissions, of a person who was assumed to be trusted and loyal. At first, it's believed as harmful actions by a trustful person not by an enemy.

Betrayal

Betrayal is in response of someone close to us who has proven untrustworthy. Most of us have felt the sting of betrayal; sadly, some of us have even inflicted it. As much as we feel a sense of sadness and or insecurity. Betrayal will cause the same effect when we do to another.

Betrayal (or backstabbing) is the breaking or violation of a presumptive contract, trust, or confidence that produces moral and psychological conflict within a relationship amongst individuals.

Action

So what do we do about it?

As Christians we must be able to retain one's trust and confidence in us as the children of God. There are obvious dangers in not overcoming the pain betrayal causes another. One may lose another's ability to trust in him/her, by becoming a betrayer in retaliation or even self-defense. We may choose not to acknowledge the betrayal and thereby expose ourselves to further hurt and emotional numbing to avoid the pain.

This will eventually lead to an inability to experience joy because it will haunt the person one day or the other, of the deplorable deed. If we happen to be the betrayer, as Christians, we must consciously know and admit the wrong done and work even through the pain, so that we might trust or be trusted again.

This way, we can find the true foundation of our security and happiness. Jesus was not immune to betrayal.

Judas, a friend whom Jesus trusted with the group's finances, for the promise of a fee betrayed Him in to be crucified. What is perhaps worse is that Judas accepted thirty pieces of silver in exchange for the life of his friend, which we can learn in Matthew 26:14-16

> "What are you willing to give me if I hand Him over to you?"

> *And they weighed out for and paid to him thirty pieces of silver [about twenty-one dollars*

> *and sixty cents]. And from that moment he sought a fitting opportunity to betray Him".*

> *What's more, Judas betrayed Jesus with a kiss of greeting: And he came up to Jesus at once and said,*

> *"Hail (greetings, good health to You, long life to You), Master!" And he embraced Him and kissed Him with [pretended] warmth and devotion. (Matthew 26:49).*

Not only did Judas accept a fee for the betrayal, he also came to Jesus greeting Him and kissed Him for the Roman guards to recognizehim. Jesus knew that Judas would betray Him, yet He chose to bring the man into His inner fellowship even for His last supper.

We can learn that Jesus called Judas "friend," even after the kiss that would lead to Jesus' arrest.

> *"Jesus said to him, Friend, for what are you here?"*

(Matthew 26:50).

On a smaller scale, Peter betrayed Jesus. The disciple who vowed to follow Jesus to death (Matthew 26:33-35), three times denied even knowing Jesus. After His resurrection, Jesus restored Peter, giving the man three opportunities to affirm his love for Jesus and confirming His trust in the disciple which we can learn from John 21:15-19.

David, too, experienced the sting of betrayal. In Psalm55:12-14 he writes,

> *"For it is not an enemy who reproaches and taunts me—then I might bear it; nor is it one who has hated me who insolently vaunts himself against me—then I might hide from him. But it was you, a man my equal, my companion and my familiar friend. We had sweet fellowship together and used to walk to the house of God in company."*

David was no stranger to the torment of enemies, but even that seemed less painful than betrayal from a friend. David's first response was to experience the pain of betrayal. He did not minimize his sense of hurt. He poured it out to God.

We, too, must acknowledge when we have been hurt … and even when we hurt others! And then we need to share that hurt with someone who understands. We might find it difficult to do so with another but God understands. Not only was Jesus betrayed in His time on earth, God has been, in a sense, betrayed by His creation.

He created us that we might glorify Him and have close relationship with Him. Instead of fellow-shipping with Him, we have betrayed him by sinned against Him, and He had to send Jesus Christ to redeem us from eternal damnation. As Christians we can know that God understands our pain … when we are pained by another's actions as well as our mental pain that remains when we betray another.

Therefore, we can pour out our pain to Him in prayer. When the betrayal is deep, it is more the reason to take it to Him without trying to sweep it under the carpet. For Christians the important step in overcoming the pain of betrayal is that of forgiveness. When we forgive someone, we are really giving ourselves a gift to be free of sinful thoughts that otherwise would plagues us.

When people intentionally inflict pain on us, our withholding of forgiveness hurts us more than it does them. As Christians we are required to forgive as Jesus Christ has taught us. We should not attempt to retaliate by betraying someone who betrayed us because we fall on to the same category.

Instead, like David did, we must learn to leave it in God's hands. David concludes his Psalm this way:

"Cast your burden on the Lord [releasing the weight of it] and He will sustain you; He will never allow the [consistently] righteous to be moved (made to slip, fall, or fail). But You, O God, will bring down the wicked into the pit of destruction; men of blood and treachery shall not live out half their days. But I will trust in, lean on, and

confidently rely on You." (Psalm55:22-23).

We must learn to leave it in God's hands. He takes care of evildoers. It is not our job to do so! Nevertheless, most importantly what we must know is that no matter what, He will take care of us!

"Cast your burden on the Lord [releasing the weight of it] and He will sustain you; He will never allow the [consistently] righteous to be moved (made to slip, fall, or fail." (Psalm55:22).

Criteria of Betrayal

Betrayals are 'non-physical' but emotional. There is no threat of serious injury or death. Instead betrayals have catastrophic effects including degradation, rejection, and humiliation. They could be life-altering but rarely life-threatening.

The range of reactions to traumatic events is wider. A perpetrator of betrayal is a traitor. A "Traitor" is a person who betrays their own political party, nation, family, friends, ethnic group, team, religion to which they belong. They could face high treason charges if its proven treason against the king is proven. On a lesser scale is the petit treason for a lesser superior.

<u>5 Categories of Betrayal</u>

- Disclosures of confidential information

- Disloyalty

- Infidelity

- Dishonest.

- Failures to offer expected assistance during significant times of need

Betrayal generates:

- Shock

- Distress

- Ruminative pre-occupation

- Self-doubt

Betrayal

- Low self-esteem

- Anger

- Punitive thoughts

- Disbelief

The psychiatric complications of betrayal include:

- Depression

- Numbness

- Denial

- Panic

- Anxiety

- Lack of self-confidence

- Unhappiness

- Sadness

- Anger

- Avoidance

- Negative appraisal of self

- Hurt

Catastrophic betrayals produce Post-Traumatic Stress Disorder (PTSD) like symptoms, in addition to Obsessive Compulsive Disorder (OCD). The bond of trust is breached and replaced by a barrier that tends to be permanent when betrayal is long lasting

A re construct only occurs during therapy and when the betrayed person acquires new information that disconfirms what happened. The seriousness of any betrayal depends on the interaction between the significance and depth of the trusting bond, and/or the magnitude of the harm caused.

"How different our lives are when we really know what is deeply important to us, and keeping that picture in our mind, we manage ourselves each day to be and do what really matters most."

Stephen Covey

Chapter 2

Betrayal Blindness

"You can't believe it happened again. Why do you keep giving him/her the benefit of the doubt? You keep wanting to hope that he/she will change but you dig a little deeper and you keep finding more lies.

You don't think he/she is capable of telling you the truth. 'God, what else don't you know?' You are not sure you can stomach digging for more, pushing him/her to tell you the truth, only to find a new low that you have hit as a couple."

Isn't this a typical conversation you yourself in while

trying to reconcile and heal with your spouse or significant other, especially when you discover an affair that has been going on for a while? It is destroying to find out that your partner lied about continued contact with the affair partner and also find out there could have been other inappropriate "friendships" with other men or women.

Previous to recent marital crisis, clients would have been described by many as an extremely intelligent, grounded, strong-minded, and secure persons - someone who would never fall victim to such a cliché ruse.

Their "shell-shock" along with the shaming self-talk of "How did I not know this was happening? How could I be so blindly trusting and stupid?" can all be chalked up to one phenomenon: Betrayal Blindness.

Aesthetics of Betrayal

Research psychologist, Jennifer Freyd, in her books 'Betrayal Trauma: The Logic of Forgetting Childhood Abuse (1996)' and 'Blind to Betrayal: Why We Fool ourselves that We Aren't Being Fooled (2013)' coined betrayal blindness. The term stemmed from her research on childhood abuse and then expanded to another form of relational betrayal trauma: infidelity.

Dr. Freyd was intrigued when she found story after story of infidelity where everyone seemed to know the partner was cheating, except for the spouse. However, in retrospect, the spouse could recount numerous, obvious signs of her partner's suspicious activities that she "didn't see" or quickly accepted her partner's false justifications surrounding the behaviors (i.e., Gas lighting). Freyd was intrigued by the victims of betrayal trauma seemingly choosing to ignore that they were being lied to, abused, or betrayed.

'Why', you ask, *'would one choose to ignore being victimized by lies, abuse, or betrayal'?*

Freyd explains,

> *"Everyday betrayal blindness is all around us. It is the systematic filtering of reality in order to*

> *maintain human relationships. It is not knowing and not remembering the betrayals of everyday life and everyday relationships in order to protect those relationships. It includes white lies and the darker lies we tell ourselves so as not to threaten our bonds. It is not seeing that your intimate partner is having an affair when others see it plainly (193)."*

Various forms of betrayal happen around us all of the time.

When we don't care about the betrayer (i.e., a stranger lies to us or harms us), we react by getting angry or hurt and avoiding that person or situation in the future. However, with intimate, dependent relationships where there are strong levels of emotional and logistical ties to another (i.e. a husband whom you love and is also the breadwinner and co-parent to your children), the more likely a person is to "ignore" betrayal or abuse.

The fear of losing the relationship suppresses our intuition telling us that we're being betrayed and harmed. In fact, the more the victim is dependent on the perpetrator of the betrayal, the more power the perpetrator has over the victim. Betrayal blindness is the same concept used to explain why acts of sexual abuse, domestic violence, and other abuses at the hands of loved ones often go uncovered, unacknowledged, and unchanged.

One's perception of dependency on another may be real, such as financial dependence if there are young children involved and, perhaps, for a stay-at-home mom, who feels she cannot sustain a proper lifestyle without her husband. However, the perception of dependency is often the result of past or current psychological manipulation where escape and change may be possible but the abused partner may not see those options at all due to fear.

Bottom line: Your fear-driven determination to maintain your marriage at all costs, supersedes your intuitive messages cautioning you that you are being mistreated, lied to, harmed, or abused. Therefore, you 'allows' the abuse and lies to continue for weeks, months, even years.

"If you are blind to the evidence that your intimate partner is having an affair, you may manage to keep the relationship from ending. But what sort of relationship is it, and what purpose does it serve?" (Freyd 194).

When you choose to ignore the truth of the state of your marriage, in essence, you are living a lie. Defense mechanisms such as lack of awareness, forgetting, denying, dissociating, and being less than fully connected internally may be adaptive but are ultimately tragic solutions in life.

When you choose to be blind to what's happening outside of you (i.e., your marriage and your partner), you may also be choosing to ignore what's going inside of you. The result can be preserving a fractured life—internally and externally—impoverished spiritually and socially. Keeping yourself blind to the betrayal does allow you to maintain the relationship with your spouse, but at what cost to your sense of self, quality of life, and sanity?

Betrayal blindness breeds from co-dependency. Its existence stems from an overriding reliance on the person who's perpetrating the betrayal. That's why the fear of losing a partner <u>should</u> <u>not</u> and <u>cannot</u> be considered a life-threatening consequence.

Life altering, yes.

Painful and sad, of course.

Life threatening, no.

Your partner can be a significant aspect of your life without becoming the single, most defining aspect of life. Your value and worth must exist in spite of your partner's approval and love.

After all, partners, like everyone else, are imperfect and act of their own free-will. You do not have control of your partner's choices or behaviors. Sure, you can influence him/her at times. However, they will ultimately do what they want and for their own reasons.

Assuming you have any control over another is a recipe for exhaustion, anger, resentment, and betrayal blindness. Your intuition, "better judgment", and sense of self are all compromised when you allow yourself to be co-dependent. In order to prevent patterns of betrayal blindness, you must work hard to empower your intuition, maintain a strong sense of self, and maintain many meaningful facets of your life beyond your primary relationship.

Freyd and Birrell emphasize in their book, Blind to Betrayal: Why We Fool Ourselves We Aren't Being Fooled, that unawareness is useful when information is too dangerous to know. Being blind to betrayal protects us. Our status quo remains the same if we do not know, and making hard decisions is put off for a while. There is a downside to being blind.

We risk being re-victimized and we risk a loss of self-esteem. Others can be victimized if we do not speak of the betrayal. Shame plays a part in keeping us silent.

Telling others is risky, but you take back your power when you do. There is a chance for hope and justice when you speak. Betrayal blindness is not seeing what is in front of your face. Others can see what you do not.

Freyd and Birrell write that "betrayal blindness requires being in the dual state of simultaneously knowing and not knowing something important." The mind does not process the information correctly because the losses are too overwhelming at the time. You need to see the world as a safe place.

You need to trust people and also need stability in your life. It makes sense for you to block awareness. When children are betrayed, it is usually by being abandoned and left helpless, being rejected, or someone withdrawing love.

Betrayal means to a child,"*I am not important, I am a zero in the eyes of others.*" Freyd and Birrell state that the child handles betrayal by turning the blame inward and blaming him/herself or not allowing him/herself to be consciously aware something is happening. This allows the child to remain attached to the abuser.

"Betrayal blindness often occurs in couples where one is unfaithful to the other", writes Freyd and Birrell.

To know is to disrupt the marriage, damage the security of the family, and destroy trust. To know you've been betrayed is wanting to withdraw or confront the betrayer.

Domestic violence in the home can make these reactions risky. Freyd and Birrell state that betrayal blindness also occurs in institutions and society. Some examples I can think of are: working at a job where your contract is not honored, or being harassed by your boss or another employee.

To speak up may mean losing your job, making others angry, or to be told you are overreacting. It may be impossible to leave because you have a family to take care of, or you lack skills, so you remain silent and start being blind to survive. Another example of institutional betrayal is a child, in need of care, is sent to a foster home where she/he is sexually abused.

An example of being betrayed by the society is: You are black. You are told you have equal rights and protection under the law. You are stopped by the police while driving and when you try to explain something to them, you are shot.

Freyd and Birrell write about the reasons why betrayal trauma is so hard to recover from and how it leaves you with wounds that can last a life-time. The victim deals with the trauma of the event as well as the trauma that occurs to a person's sense of safety and security, and self-esteem. A victim's value system is torn upside down and everything he/she once believed was true is proved to be untrue.

Betrayal attacks the very foundation that makes you who you are. It damages your body, your mind, and your spiritual wellbeing. For a child, a parent is there to attend to his/her needs and do for him/her what he/she cannot do for him/herself.

Betrayal: A Child's Perspective

A parent's job is to love a child, brag on him/her, be reliable, and trust worthy. A parent teaches a child all about good relationship skills, that the world is a safe place most of the time, and goodness can be found around him/her. This builds the basic building blocks for a successful life.

When a child is sexually abused, his/her sense of security, safety, trust, reliability, goodness, and self-identity is severely damaged. The child learns that pain occurs often for no good reason, that no one cares for his/her needs, that he/she needs to be watchful and protect him/herself any way he/she can, that he/she is there to take care of the needs of others, that his/her body is not his/hers, that evil exists in his/her world and in his/her place of refuge, and he/she is told to not tell, and/or to not cry by the abuser.

Down inside, he/she knows something is wrong so

the child blames him/herself for not being good enough, for not being smart enough, or strong enough to get away. It must all be his/her fault. Somehow, he/she messed up or this wouldn't be happening to him/her.

A child's perception of his/her external and internal reality becomes not only distorted but also confusing. If he/she can't get away physically, the child will take his/her mind some place away from the abuse. There is damage done to the body and the normal development of his/her sexuality. It would make sense if he/she feels depressed, anxious, has poor self-esteem, feels confused, acts out his/her anger and fear, and can't trust anyone.

It makes sense that in order to protect oneself, the child would not withdraw or confront his/her abuser who is bigger and allocates the resources he/she needs to keep alive. To deny his/her reality and to forget what has happened helps him/her remain safe. Its lowers the anxiety.

No child wants to see his/her parent or caregiver as a monster because that would make them a monster too, so he/she thinks. There is safety in denial, forgetting, dissociation, and other defensive mechanisms a child can use. The drawback to this, Freyd and Birrell write, is the abused may not be able to discuss the injustice if they continue to forget and deny what happened to them. Freyd and Birrell define betrayal blindness as" not seeing, systematically, important instances of treachery and injustice being done which ultimately results in negative consequences."

Rotating in and Out of Betrayal Blindness: Tamara

In many ways, Tamara had an idyllic childhood: two loving parents at home; family game nights with mom, dad, aunties, uncles, and cousins; good grades and loads of friends at school.

Hers was the house in the neighborhood where all the other kids wanted to sleep over. In the daytimes of her childhood, she knew she was special. In the nighttime, well, she knew she was special too, but in a different way.

Her father began molesting her when she was very young and by middle childhood was regularly raping her. During these assaults, she'd float away and escape to a safe place in her mind. During the days, she enjoyed a life of love with all her family, including her father.

Once Tamara left home at age 18, her awareness of incest fluctuated dramatically, as if she were on a merry-go-round, rotating around her experiences of trauma. Sometimes, aware that her father had betrayed her, she faced the reality of sexual abuse in her family with tremendous pain, depression, and anxiety.

At other times she denied her experience of abuse by forgetting, free to appreciate all the wonderful aspects of her childhood, while being blind to the incest. As an adult, Tamara's betrayal blindness protected her from the pain of knowing her father had sexually abused her, just as it had in childhood.

However, her presence on this merry-go-round of rotating betrayal blindness also structured her possibilities for growth. Moreover, it prevented her from moving toward a deeper, more integrative healing from trauma.

In this way, she stayed stuck for years, the rate of the rotation in and out of betrayal blindness dependent upon the situation: present-day vacation with family - blind to historical betrayal; dinners with her best friend - awareness of incest; entering a sexual relationship with a man - quick rotation from awareness back to betrayal blindness.

Although a healthy body, supportive relationships, and the opportunity to make safe disclosures may help an individual come to terms with trauma (as explained in Blind to Betrayal), integrating the knowledge that one has been betrayed by a trusted other rarely proceeds in a linear fashion. More often, individuals like Tamara—and those bearing witness to the trauma of others—rotate in and out of betrayal blindness on their journey to make sense of the past, find words for their experience, and heal.

Overt examples of rotating betrayal blindness like Tamara's may be common amongst those who have experienced betrayal trauma, but this phenomenon can also manifest itself in more subtle ways. For example, even when traumatic events are explicitly remembered and disclosed, individuals may minimize their significance by dismissing the event as unimportant or otherwise engaging in what Mic Hunter describes as "bargaining" with the self.

For example, an adult survivor of childhood sexual abuse who suddenly remembers the incest might insist: "it couldn't have been abuse because Dad was such a family man."

Likewise, an individual whose lover committed infidelity might say to themselves "Yes, but it only happened once" or "Yes, but she was hurting and unable to make good decisions."

Betrayal

Such statements are often interspersed with stronger aversive reactions to the betrayals in question. In this way, individuals may use rotating betrayal blindness to maintain the coherence of their autobiographical memory without letting go of denial that a betrayal has occurred.

While more research is needed to understand how and why rotating betrayal blindness occurs, it is clear that the degree to which memories of betrayal remain available over time (something Severs and colleagues refer to as memory persistence) fluctuates—often dramatically—even long after discovering and disclosing memories of abuse.

The very nature of trauma may help us make sense of this phenomenon. By definition, betrayal does not fit cleanly within the confines of an individual's expectations, but rather, unexpectedly disrupts one's experience of relational and narrative continuity. As such, betrayal poses a threat to the individual's experience of close others as safe and predictable.

This may be especially true for children. Their experience (and by extension understanding) of the world is more limited than adults' and they depend on adults to scaffold their experiences of the world.

As Robyn Fivush explains in "The Development of Autobiographical Memory," although younger children are able to connect past events with their present self, research from developmental psychology suggests that it is only in middle childhood that one's life narrative begins to emerge. As such, children who experience betrayal in early childhood may have a particularly difficult time constructing a coherent narrative of the trauma.

However, even for adults, relational betrayals may be so incongruous with their beliefs about relationships with trusted others that recognizing and naming betrayal is extraordinarily difficult—requiring significant narrative reorganization to maintain a coherent sense of self. Given the discontinuity between betrayal and the rest of an individual's experience, it is perhaps not surprising that trauma memories often emerge in unexpected ways.

In the case of flashbacks, awareness of the trauma violently intrudes into the individual's experience, as a betrayal is suddenly remembered, triggered by a touch, sound, or smell that reminds them of the event. By contrast, awareness of the betrayal may emerge slowly, as though through a fog.

And these two experiences may occur within the same individual—even simultaneously—for the same trauma. In either case, the process of integrating trauma memories necessarily resists a linear course, and may entail what Johnathan Schooler describes as "changes in the individual's meta-awareness of the abuse".

The Trauma of Betrayal

Betrayal trauma occurs when the betrayer is the person upon whom the victims rely for satisfaction of a need necessary for continued wellbeing. An example of betrayal trauma is childhood physical, emotional, or sexual abuse."

Both victims and perpetrators report a range of negative emotions. The victim experiences disgust, anxiety, and shame. On the other hand, the perpetrators experience guilt, self-disgust, regret, and remorse.

Relationship Betrayal and Trauma

Relationship betrayal is one of the most painful human experiences. The resulting trauma refers to the damage that is caused when someone experiences a betrayal in their primary relationship that damages the trust, safety and security of the bond they have with their partner. Discovering that someone you trusted has deeply hurt you pulls the reality rug out from under your feet.

A damaging aspect of betrayal is that your sense of reality is undermined. What felt like solid trust suddenly crumbles. Your innocence is shattered. You are left wondering;

'What happened?'

Betrayal

'How could this happen?'

'Who is this person?'

The way that we bond to our spouses is a profound puzzle. It is a process of intertwining our lives, having children together and creating memories, we become more and more interdependent with one another. This is not codependency. This is healthy, normal, mutual dependency.

It is what makes relationships function, providing safety and security. However, when that attachment is breached or damaged it affects your physical, mental, emotional and spiritual health in deeply painful ways.

Instead of grounding you, it puts you in free fall. Instead of security you experience fear. Because your spouse is the source of your pain, they now feel like a threat to your well-being; a danger rather than a safe haven or a source of comfort and rest.

Betrayal puts you in a situation where you need to

discern what's best for you. It's complicated. Perhaps love is still alive and your partner admits his or her mistake and expresses remorse.

Would it be a courageous risk to give your partner another chance or a foolish mistake to trust again? Rather than act impulsively, you may serve yourself by taking time to sort out your feelings and find some clarity about what's best for you, your relationship and your family.

Understanding the chaos

The shocking discovery of betrayal in marriage induces feelings of chaos, confusion, and debilitating despair. Betrayal creates such intense emotions for the afflicted spouse that the memories and trauma may remain for months, even years.

Betrayal trauma is a condition that parallels the symptoms of PTSD (post-traumatic stress disorder) and is caused when someone experiences betrayal and deception within their primary relationship; this betrayal damages the trust and safety of the relationship and calls into question the bond they have with their partner. You may experience tremendous anxiety, high stress, fatigue, depression, despair, grief, fear, and other serious symptoms.

<u>First Steps</u>

The first steps to responding to the chaos that has consumed your life is to understand the nature of addiction and to find support. Dealing with a partner's sexual addiction can feel different than other addiction. It can feel like all the winds and storms are coming directly at you; it feels like it is a personal attack.

<u>Your Feelings are Completely Normal</u>

While the trauma from betrayal is real, it's possible to heal. With helpful support, you can take steps to reveal vulnerable feelings that lie beneath the initial anger and outrage. Your heart can be made whole, your life can be made brighter, and you can ultimately be released from the sting of betrayal and its accompanied trauma. Counseling offers a safe place to reveal feelings, work through grief and anger, uncover longstanding issues and provide helpful support and guidance.

The Stages of Trauma

<u>Shock</u>

This stage is the initial discovery of your partner's betrayal and deceit. This new information may cause you to engage in extreme behavior, depending on your individual nature and personality. While many lash out, others shut down in response to the tragic reveal. Loss of composure is a natural physical and emotional reaction.

<u>Denial</u>

Denial follows shock in part because you are unable to fully comprehend and grasp what has happened. It all seems improbable that your intimate relationship has been impaired by your trusted partner. Your disbelief and desire for it all to just go away can lead you to reject the reality of your

Betrayal

partner's betrayal.

<u>Obsession</u>

Once the realness of the situation begins to settle, you soon find it difficult to remain focused on anything other than your partner's deceit and betrayal. You begin to wonder and fear over all possible, detailed deception practiced by your spouse, and you examine if there was any truth to your relationship at all. You analyze and question yourself, investigating upon something you might have changed to prevent this damage from occurring. You are caught in a cyclone of painful details and frenzied analysis concerning yourself, your partner, and the relationship you have together.

<u>Anger</u>

Recognizing your behavior has little or no impact upon your partner's behavior, you become enraged with the profound pain your partner's choices have caused. In moments, it feels as if you partner has intentionally injured you and your relationship, leaving you with heated anger. This is an incredibly normal response, even if uncharacteristic to your personality.

<u>Bargaining</u>

As your anger tones down, you start to look forward in wonderment at life ahead.

Where might you go from here?

What is in the future?

If you have children together, how do you continue as a family?

These thoughts and questions begin to weigh heavy within you. Bargaining, compromising your personal wellness, even the thought of excusing some bad behavior from your spouse, may suddenly seem less daunting than heading into the vast unknown. However, neglecting to attend to the true damage in your relationship, you will inevitably be led towards further damage and devastation down the road.

Betrayal

Depression

This stage may be considered the wild card of all the stages, because it can take place simultaneously with all of the other stages. Life feels dark and everyday living has become harder and harder to handle. What once brought you joy, no longer seems to excite you.

You, yourself, may even begin to engage in unhealthy behavior as a method of coping or as a distraction from your despair. Overall, you are feeling fragmented, broken, and are losing hope with life; the reality of your situation feels beyond your capacity to bear.

Acceptance

At this point you are able to acknowledge and honestly accept the reality of what has happened and are ready to take action and find a way to move forward. This stage is one of courage. It is recognizing that something has been broken and cannot stay the same.

Whether moving in step with your partner or alone, you understand the process ahead will be hard. But you are ready to feel emotionally, mentally and physically healthy again.

*"Unless you can find some sort of loyalty,
you cannot find unity and peace in your
active living."*

Josiah Royce

Chapter 3

Betrayal and Shame

During healing, rotating betrayal blindness could perhaps be described as the dialectic between a self's fidelity to the event of trauma, on the one hand, and a self's bearing witness to that event, on the other.

For some, concurrent denial and awareness help protect the individual from one truth of trauma, while helping them integrate others.

That is, denial itself can be conceptualized as a sort of fidelity to the event of trauma: it signifies the unallowable nature of what has happened. In some cases, it reflects direct instruction by a betrayer to forget or disbelieve personal experience.

True healing begins when this rotating motion takes an individual beyond the *merry-go-round*, which only spins in place. Rotating betrayal blindness often persists into a phase that we can call the *upward healing spiral*—a process that leads the individual toward fuller integration of trauma and its ongoing effects on their life.

In this phase, however, rotating betrayal blindness occurs within a larger narrative frame of recovery from trauma. Here, denial and awareness still co-construct the meaning of traumatic events for the individual. In contrast to the merry-go-round phase, however, where they alternate without going anywhere new, in the upward healing spiral, the rotating elements of denial and awareness drive integration and foster meaningfully new experiences.

As a child, Tamara was completely dependent on her parents for survival and denied that her father was sexually abusing her at night. During these years, betrayal blindness helped her survive and protected her from immense psychological pain. Once Tamara had left home and became financially independent, she slowly began to remember the incest.

However, remembering was hardly a linear process, and she often doubted whether her memories were real. Sometimes Tamara couldn't remember the sexual abuse at all. For years she lived on a merry-go-round of rotating betrayal blindness, stuck oscillating between blindness to the immense betrayal of her father's actions and awareness of the abuse.

Without an overarching narrative frame of recovery from trauma, this process of alternation between denial and awareness kept Tamara stuck. However, by putting words to her experience and sharing her memories with trusted others, Tamara made a decision to step off of the merry-go-round and begin a healing journey where betrayal blindness played a new and important role—taking her beyond survival and helping her grow.

While it may seem counterintuitive that denial could aid in healing, rotating betrayal blindness—when operating within a context of recovery—helps people like Tamara integrate the reality of betrayal and move forward with their lives.

According to Jennifer Freyd's betrayal trauma theory victims of traumatic events involving betrayal by a close other are more likely to forget the abuse compared to victims of events perpetrated by strangers. They are also more likely to dissociate from awareness of the abuse. That is, they may disconnect from their own thoughts, feelings, or behaviors related to the abusive events.

Effects of betrayal

Perhaps no action in life stings more than betrayal. To feel betrayed, you have to trust someone enough to be hurt by their unexpected actions. Recovering from this hurt can leave you unwilling to trust anyone in the same way for a long time.

The psychological effects of betrayal are broad, even

affecting the stability of societies. Trust is a basis for human existence, influenced by certain chemicals in the brain, such as oxytocin, a body chemical that accelerates trustful feelings. When going through your own betrayal, you can experience many related emotions.

You may experience:

- Shock

- Grief

- Anger

- Isolation

- Sadness

- Depression

- Feelings of degradation

- Humiliation, worthlessness.

- The betrayer becomes a source of

contamination

Shock

The initial feeling most people experience when encountering a betrayal is shock. You're likely to spend weeks, months or even years in disbelief that the person who offended you was capable of her actions. Often times, trust is built over time and, based on witnessed behaviors, it takes time to reprogram your brain about the nature of this person's character.

Anger

After it settles in that your friend is capable of such a derogatory action, you are likely to experience some level of anger. It's common to get mad about letting yourself trust a person who was so insensitive and be furious at the betrayer. You may even have vengeful feelings of wanting to get back at that person, or hurt him in the same way he hurt you.

Grief

After the more caustic feelings of shock and anger dissipate, you may experience classic feelings of grief. If the betrayal is so great that you lose your relationship entirely, you may grieve that loss. You may also grieve what you thought you had with this person, which can be more difficult than letting go of something that actually existed.

Isolation

If feelings of betrayal encroach greatly upon your sense of well-being, you may want to isolate yourself from others. Going out with your friends or making new ones seem less and less appealing. If feelings of isolation are allowed to go on for too long, you can even develop a social phobia.

Sadness/Depression

Feelings of sadness are common after experiencing a betrayal. It hurts to have your trust in a person annihilated, and It's a logical progression of emotions to feel sad along the way. For those who don't work out their feelings and allow them to fester, they may even slip into a more precarious state of depression

Crush the Shame and Pain of Betrayal

Not knowing about the abuse can help the victim to maintain a relationship with the perpetrator. Whereas victims of trauma perpetrated by a stranger may be motivated to either fight back or run away, these responses are less helpful in the case of betrayal trauma, in which the perpetrator is providing food, shelter, and/or emotional connection to the victim.

It is also possible that feeling ashamed of oneself plays a protective function in close relationships characterized by abuse.

For example, if a parent emotionally, physically, or sexually assaults a child, the child may feel ashamed of herself instead of feeling angry at or afraid of the abuser.

Researchers such as Dacher Keltner have found that

whereas anger often results in fighting and fear often results in fleeing, shame tends to result in submitting and appeasing. Thus, the expression of shame has the potential to elicit a caregiving response from the perpetrator which could ultimately keep the victim as safe as possible within an unsafe situation.

In a study of Olympic and Paralympic athletes, Jessica Tracy and David Matsumoto found that the slumped posture and downward gaze associated with shame occur cross-culturally. A variety of factors influences the tendency to respond to a stressor with the bodily expression and/or internal experience of shame and for some survivors, the presence of an all-or-nothing thinking style.

For example, *"If I am not perfect, I am worthless"*, may contribute to the tendency to experience shame readily.

Although we propose that proneness to shame is useful for survival during ongoing abuse, it has harmful consequences in its chronic form. Bernice

Andrews has linked long-term chronic shame to depression, Jennie Leskala and colleagues have linked shame to Post-Traumatic Stress Disorder (PTSD). On the other hand, Michelle Covert and colleagues have linked shame with difficulties in interpersonal problem solving, whilst Martin Dorahy has linked shame with interpersonal disconnection, to name a few.

Research by Sally Dickerson and colleagues has also found chronic shame to be associated with physical health risks including increased risk of earlier mortality. According to research by Ananda Amstadter and Laura Vernon, chronic shame may be particularly relevant for survivors of interpersonal trauma in that shame increases over time following interpersonal trauma, but decreases over time following non-interpersonal trauma.

Accumulating shame following interpersonal trauma may be related to both the betrayal element of interpersonal trauma, and what Judith Herman has referred to as "feeling traps" that occur when the survivor feels ashamed of feeling ashamed. It is possible that shame and dissociation are two separate methods of protecting a relationship with a perpetrator who is depended-upon, or it is possible that shame and dissociation work together to facilitate survival.

The most broadly accepted theory attempting to explain the relationship between shame and dissociation posits that dissociation is a method of defending against the overwhelming pain of shame.

Shame scholars Donald Nathansan and Michael Lewis have adopted this theory. Dissenting views suggest that dissociation does not interrupt shame in betrayal trauma survivors, but instead either increases shame or does not affect it at all.

Healing takes courage and we all have courage, even if we have to dig a little to find it.

Tori Amos

Chapter 4

Hook Up

If shame indeed is a method of protecting the relationship with the perpetrator, it would not be adaptive for dissociation to interrupt shame. Victims may lose self-respect, self-worth and confidence, sometimes feel they don't matter, and that their actions have few repercussions on anyone but themselves.

They may end up in many intimate situations which were unplanned and rather random, really just sleeping around. That may sound so demeaning and harsh, yet one may not quite understand.

Why?

They seem to have fun, and feel safe during the process, and don't seem to see the problem or what the big deal is all about. Just one more guy, one more night, and one more experience.

The above illustrates the complexities of a new sexual terrain: hook up culture. Hooking up involves sexual encounters between people who are not dating each other. Although hooking up is intended to be fun, in reality there are serious risks involved.

William Flack and his colleagues found that almost one quarter of the women they surveyed were sexually assaulted during their time at college. More than three quarters of those assaults happened during hook ups.

For some women, hooking up also results in consensual but less than pleasurable sex. Although both men and women hook up in order to feel pleasure, female students are not necessarily finding that pleasure with their sexual partners.

Elizabeth Armstrong and her colleagues surveyed college students. They found that women experienced orgasm only one third as often as their male partners.

The college women William Flack and his colleagues surveyed admitted to prioritizing their hook up partners' pleasure over their own. They, potentially, agreed to sexual activities that they found uncomfortable or undesirable.

Given the high risk of sexual assault and the likelihood of receiving less pleasure than they give, why do college women hook up?

Betrayal trauma theory offers one explanation.

When a person is harmed by a close and trusted other, he or she may be more likely to forget or be unaware of the abuse than if a stranger had perpetrated it. By not fully knowing about the abuse, the individual is able to maintain an important relationship with the abuser.

In Blind to Betrayal, Jennifer Freyd and Pamela Birrell explain betrayal trauma theory and show betrayal can both do damage and also lead to betrayal blindness.

Betrayal Trauma Theory and the Hook Up Culture?

First, the student's peers may form a trusted and necessary community, then receive belonging, friendship, and romance from that community. When sexual violence happens in this tight knit social world, and particularly when the community itself enables that violence, students face a cognitive conflict.

They can be fully aware of the high prevalence of sexual assault, but that awareness comes at a high personal price. They must then live with the reality that a community they value and love creates an environment where sexual assault is likely to occur.

Furthermore, there may be additional consequences

for full awareness of violence; the community in which a student was harmed may punish her both subtly and explicitly for speaking about sexual assault. Considering the important ways in which students derive belonging, friendship, and potential romance from their community, these consequences are profound.

Betrayal trauma theory suggests it may be adaptive for a student to remain unaware of the ways in which her community permits and even encourages assault. Without awareness of this betrayal, students can remain strongly identified community members and believe that a college student needs to explore sex, love, and relationships. Remaining blind to betrayal allows her to continue to engage in hook up culture.

And students often view hook up culture as the only viable pathway to both pleasure and romance on college campuses.

Betrayal blindness offers an explanation for why college women continue to hook up despite the high prevalence of sexual assault. William Flack and his colleagues found that almost one third of the college women they interviewed who hooked up had experienced unwanted intercourse.

In comparison, women who never hooked up reported zero incidences of unwanted intercourse. Hook up culture clearly plays a role in high rates of sexual assault on college campuses. Yet students feel empowered by hooking up; women in particular may see hooking up as a way to seize control of their sexuality as newly independent adults.

But simultaneously, hook up culture also produces an environment where students are highly motivated to remain unaware of underlying misogyny, norms that prioritize male pleasure, and high rates of sexual coercion and assault. Think back to the victim earlier quoted who describes the dark side of hooking up: having lost self-respect, self-worth and confidence, but moments later, plaintively asks the reader to understand why she continues to hook up:

"What's the big deal about one more guy, one more night, one more experience?"

The inconsistency in these two statements illustrates a form of blindness. This is the way this student continues to survive in her community without seeing her own pain.

In a culture where awareness of violence comes with consequences, students or anyone for that matter hook up without full knowledge of the risks and realities. Blindness to betrayal serves a purpose, but it is also an obstacle to;

- Pleasure

- Consent

- Empowerment

Surprisingly, these are the core things young women seek when they hook up in the first place.

Stab the body and it heals, but injure the heart and the wound lasts a lifetime.

Mineko Iwasaki

Chapter 5

The Impact of Betrayal

Trust and goodwill are the fuel for healthy relationships. It's very important to have confidence that family members and spouses are honest with each other.

But what happens to a relationship when a relative or spouse betrays your trust?

How can family members heal?

How do these infidelities impact intimate relationships?

I frequently hear about husbands or wives who run up huge credit card bills or who have big gambling losses that they hide from each other.

Joy, an impulse shopper, had credit cards with $20,000 balances that her husband John didn't know about. One day, he found out accidentally, when he received a call from a credit card company. He was shocked and had no idea that Joy had a secret life.

Benson was having a long-term affair with a co-worker. His wife had suspected that he was involved in a relationship, but he denied it, and she chose to believe him. He insisted that he wasn't seeing anyone. But when the truth came out, his wife was crushed. Not just because he was having an affair, but also because he had been dishonest about it.

One Christmas holiday, Joan, 20 years of age, learned from a cousin that her father wasn't her "real" father. Her mother had an affair and became pregnant. It caused huge upheaval, and her mother had told her sister, who later told her son. Joan was shattered when she heard the story from her cousin.

Long-term effects of great betrayals bring sadness for everyone. The individuals who do the betraying often have an easier time moving on. Filled with shame and regret, they know what they were doing, even though they make poor choices.

They can move forward and re-invent themselves as more honest individuals. They can start anew.

Our culture "has a soft spot for the prodigal sons and daughters who set about repairing their ways. Talk shows thrive on these tales. It's never too late to start anew.

Frequently, we hear their impatience with the victims of their betrayal.

Why can't they move on?

Why can't they let go of the past?

Why can't they live today?

Betrayal

"I'm sorry!" they say, *"I didn't mean to hurt you so badly. It will never happen again."*

Why doesn't their partner believe them? Especially, when they are so certain that they will never make these bad choices again? But it's so much more difficult for the victims of betrayal.

They blame themselves for not knowing what was going on, for believing their partner, or for being blind to the clues that they now realize were all around them.

How could they have been so trusting? How could they have been so naïve?

There is also the tendency to compulsively rehash everything that happened in the past.

Who else knew?

Has my husband told me the whole truth?

Did other family members know this secret?

In addition to intense feelings of humiliation and shame, they feel stupid. Friends and family may also suggest that they were responsible for missing what is now obvious. It's very hard to "get over" these betrayals.

It changes everything forever. Once trust is so grievously broken, it can never go back to its previous shape or form. There are scars that do not go away.

The relationship is forever changed. These experiences are traumatic, not just because they are so painful, but because they change the victim's life story. Their view of the world is altered.

Hard Questions

Forgiveness may come, but don't expect to ever forget what happened.

Others may want you to "forgive and forget", but amnesia is not possible or desirable! Don't pressure your relative or spouse to "move on" or "let go."

Betrayal

That just rubs salt in the wound.

Avoid rehashing the past.

A plain fact - love is blind!

You may never know every detail of what happened. Sometimes, forgiveness is not possible. Spouses may "want" to forgive their partner, but find they can't. That is often the result of infidelity.

Have you experienced a betrayal?

How has it impacted you?

In another scenario, how do you explain that to a child growing up that they are from an egg donor and avoid the secret?

It's important to talk to them as soon as they can understand the birds and bees. It's not a good idea to put it off.

There is never an easy time to tell kids about their origins. Kids hate it when they find out when they are older. What happens when the betrayal is your own government?

What happens when you deal with the most corrupt insurance company? I am powerless to stop what takes place behind a closed door and the people who turn a blind eye to what takes place every day in our state. It can be drowning.

"Instead of looking for a person who checks all the boxes, focus on a person with whom you can imagine yourself writing a story with that entails edits and revisions."

Esther Perel

Chapter 6

Is It Possible to Heal After Betrayal?

Betrayal is a breaking of trust and goodwill in a relationship through some form of wounding. Depending on the circumstances, it can take a long time to heal from and can leave us changed forever.

Betrayal has broken marriages, ended long term friendships and has been the cause of family rifts that can span generations. It may be through a sudden event that can leave us feeling shocked and in disbelief, as in the discovery of an infidelity or an affair.

Alternatively, it may be experienced over time, through a series of lies or indiscretions that gradually deteriorate our confidence, trust and respect. Whether it's our good friend, partner, work colleague, sibling or parent, many of us have experienced the specific wounding that is felt from betrayal.

We know how this type of wounding needs sensitive handling, patience and loving repair for recovery.

How Do You Get Betrayed?

The sting of betrayal may be experienced through;

- A broken promise

- A breaking of confidentiality

- Feeling abandoned by family or friends during a life's struggle

- Seeing someone else getting the long awaited pay-raise we felt we deserved

- Worse still, if a promotion simply passes over your head

Right?

Whatever your experience of betrayal, it usually involves a mixture of feelings – hurt, bruised, angry, resentful, anxious, and deeply disappointed.

Some of the effects of a betrayal include:

- losing a partner or close friend

- lowering self-confidence or self-esteem, questioning your ability to trust and feel close to others

- fear around opening your heart to others

- affecting intimacy and closeness to others

It is a common experience for people who've been betrayed to say that they saw some of the signs beforehand. It may have been a felt sense that something was wrong, a gut feeling. You can often diminish these because part of you really doesn't want to believe they're true.

You want to give your trust to the person that you know and believe in their highest good.

Why Does Betrayal Happen?

Given that we are all dealing with our own motivations, blind spots, wounds, ego needs, reactions and impulses it shouldn't really come as a surprise that people will fail us. Alternatively, that there will be times that we will inevitably fail people we know and love. No matter how sensitive we might want to be, it is part of our humanness, our growth and maturation to make mistakes.

Taking ownership of hurt we've caused is an opportunity for us to know ourselves better and create healing from our own pasts. Most of us don't consciously set out to hurt someone when they feel betrayed by us. It is often something we've done out of our unconsciousness.

The betrayal or 'let down' can be a wakeup call around consciously looking at and taking responsibility around our behaviour which is the first step for creating change.

Someone Close

I had been working with a client around her feeling of betrayal by her mother. It deeply affected her ability to trust or be close to her mother and her relationships with her women friends.

Growing up, she never felt acknowledged or protected by her mother around her father's explosive, abusive behaviour. Her mother always seemed to dismiss or diminish her hurt and take her father's side, no matter how poorly she was treated. This, in some ways, was more painful for her than her father's abuse towards her.

Despite repeatedly feeling betrayed by her mother she still longed for a close relationship with her and hoped one day her mother would see and understand how she felt.

Over time, she had to face the difficulty that this wasn't so. Not because she didn't deserve it, but because of a limitation in her mother, not being able to shift her focus of compassion towards her daughter.

The 4 Step Process to Get Healed from Betrayal

Healing the Hurt

The first step for healing to occur was for my client to stop expecting her mother to behave differently – given that this was consistently her mother's behaviour. Every time she attempted to have a conversation with her mother about past hurts she would become defensive, dismiss her experience and my client would feel hurt all over again.

When we looked at her family history, it wasn't surprising to see that her mother had her own deep, unresolved issues around intimacy. Much of what my client was taking on board as being unlovable was not about her personally but her mother's own wounds. This was the start for her to really see the mother she had, rather than the mother she kept longing for, which is really all that we need to acknowledge for us to heal from hurt.

Grieving, Feeling the Disappointment

To stop expecting her mother to respond differently also helped her get in touch with the deep disappointment she held around having the sort of mother who would really support her. A great deal of grief arose around the closeness and understanding that she longed for with her mother.

Allowing yourself to feel our grief and acknowledging its presence takes the focus off those who betray you and back to yourself. As you do this, you start listening to and giving loving attention to your hurts.

This starts your own tender compassion for yourself. It gives you the nurture and attention you deserved.

Validating and Loving our Authentic Experience

Getting better at listening to and validating your own needs helps you take care of yourself better. You also start to catch the times when you would diminish or dismiss your experiences or internally criticize yourself.

You start to really listen closely to the needs of your inner self that need validation, support, understanding and protection. Over time, the betrayal you had initially felt now becomes the doorway to creating your own healing.

You start giving to yourself that which you so deeply long for from significant others. As you become more practiced at this, your need for validation from your significant other(s) diminishes.

Forgiving and Letting Go

In the process of letting go of the type of needs you want from others, you start to see much more clearly who you really had. This allows you to appreciate some of your significant other's specific strengths and positive qualities. You also start to practice stronger boundaries around your relationships that make life easier for you.

Knowing there are limitations in where you can go around your intimacy, this may take time and patience. Practicing listening to your feelings, trusting them, and responding to them.

"Live by your own rules. Move to your rhythm, instead of dancing to the beat of someone else's drum. Decide how you want to be treated. Choose what you will or will not tolerate. Leave if you don't get what you want."

Sherry Argov

Chapter 7

The 5 Steps to Break the Cycle of Betrayal

Is There Recovery After Betrayal?

Getting over hurt requires recovery time. It is unrealistic to expect to get over feeling your grief and hurt quickly. Recovery time means listening to your heart and allowing it to stay soft despite having been hurt.

What Do You Do When You've Been Betrayed?

Here are some 5 steps to break the cycle of betrayal with key questions to help assess things for yourself.

1. Has the betrayal you've experienced been a shock, something out of the blue, or has there been an ongoing deterioration of goodwill, disrespect of boundaries, conflict, small lies?

2. What, if anything, do you feel you need from the other person in order to gain some peace and closure? If they are unable or unwilling to do this how can you seek this for yourself elsewhere?

3. What support and guidance do you need for this to occur? Do you need to talk to someone to ensure that you get this fulfilled or to decide what to do?

4. Where might you be dismissing or diminishing your own feelings of hurt, anger, fear or caution? In order to keep a balance between an open heart and a clear head. Are you paying more attention to your feelings, thoughts and

intuition?

5.   Who is around you that you can trust and speak to? Friends, family members or professional help through counselling, social work, or GP.

Listening to your heart and allowing it to guide you helps to recover your trust in your inner self. When you are hurt, you cannot make the pain go away or change what happened.

You can, however, reach out and get support and comfort from people you love – friends or family members. It can also be a good time to reach out for help from an experienced counsellor. For a free 30 minutes counseling session, let's connect on Instagram (a)askaleen.

"Loyalty is from above; betrayal is from below."

Bob Sorge

THE END

Acknowledgements

Foremost, I thank Almighty God most of all. For without Almighty God, I would not be able to do any of this.

I am grateful to my family members for standing with me during my career and helping support my efforts in writing of this book. Thank you for always making me smile and for understanding on those weekend mornings when I was writing this book instead of playing games. I hope that one day they can read this book and understand why I spent so much time in front of my computer.

I express special thanks to the technical team for their

patience, guidance, enthusiastic encouragement, and useful critique from the start to the finish of this book. Their valuable support and professional guidance in keeping the progress of the work on schedule helped me in finalizing the book within a limited period.

I want to thank EVERYONE who said anything positive to me and /or taught me something. It all meant something.

Thank you for everything. I have faith that this book and the subsequent ones will be great assets to the society.

About the Author

Ana Leen empowers couples and individuals to overcome personal obstacles and to improve their relationships. She has been through her over thirty years of experience in a happy marriage that has been a great resource to her and others. Using clinically tested and evidenced-based interventions, Ana has worked with over 100 couples since 2008 in her practice.

A regular guest in churches, schools, small and large groups, she also coaches and mentors the young and adults in human sexuality. She discusses various relationship and sexual topics in bridal shower and also makes presentations to local counseling professionals on how to address their clients' sexual issues.

Ana is a mental health counselor, marriage and family therapist and sex therapist, as well as a qualified counselor and supervisor. She has a Master's degree in Counselling Psychology, a

Bachelor's degree in Psychology, Counselor Education and Supervision, specializing in Life Skills training both formally and informally, Rehabilitation and Mental Health Counseling, and a Certificate in Marriage and Family Therapy.

Research shows that unhealthy relationships can cause both emotional and physical stress, whereas healthy relationships can enhance and improve overall well-being. You will find Ana offering relationship counseling, sex therapy and individual counseling for anxiety, depression and relationship issues. She is currently a Counselor of a School, and doubles up as a Research Project Coordinator, examination committee board member, and curriculum development expert among others.

Learn more about Ana and interact with her on Twitter (at)LeenGoTo.

Testimonials

I cannot tell you how much I love this. - Kelsey W.

Hooking up is a choice. Being assaulted is not a choice. - J.

Wow! I really love this one, keep it up. - L. U. T.

This is proper. - Loren W

"Don't you want your power back?' I never felt more powerful or in control than when I went through a hook up phase. I could do what I want, when I want. I could go home to my dog and my job and not have to worry about a thing. I never had regret. - Jess

Ana is a gem. Serious in her faith in The LORD, hard-

working, honest, focused and courageous. She is not easily intimidated. She stands for what she believes in without fear or favour and totally committed in all she sets out to do. Ana is a prayer warrior with deep passion to carry out the agenda of The LORD, full of patience, and understanding with an amazing personality. She does not judge you for negative things/experiences/situations in your life but gives you hope of new beginning in Christ Jesus. Love. - Shiz

Her counseling services and prayers in my family occasions are never taken for granted. I thank her for the words of wisdom during my daughter's bridal shower who says she learnt many wise and Christian lessons to help her in her marriage. Ana Leen is friendly and I would not hesitate to recommend anyone seeking counseling services to her. I have not only benefited from her in my personal growth in Christ, but also rich messages of encouragement and phone calls that can never be taken for granted. May the Lord continue to bless her as she helps others to heal? God's blessings. - Makandi R.

Ana Leen has been such a wonderful counselor to many young couples especially those doing bridal showers. She advices them on future expectations and how to handle difficult moments, pain, shame, stigma, and trauma in life. Kudos to the good work she has done to me and many other courting couples. Her strong character and word of advice keeps me moving in my marriage for the last 18 years. - Jessica

Having known Ana Leen for over 10 years, I am thoroughly impressed and confident with her ability to listen, advice, and guide you through the issues of life. For example, in marriage, work, relationship, self, and spiritual when in need of advice. – Joyce.

I have known Ana Leen close to 20 years. We once lived in the same neighborhood. She is that sort of person who works well with others irrespective of their religion, social background, and age. Ana is both friendly and courteous. For as long as I have known her, she has proven to be trustworthy, courageous, ambitious and, a very dedicated go-getter. Moreover, she is also studious and can read many kind of materials. When Ana began counseling classes and pursued her studies with a passion and dedication that was extraordinary: all the way up to mastering in Psychology. Not forgetting that she was a wife, mother and an employee. She juggled through all these, a secret she only can tell to other women to emulate. Notwithstanding, Ana has excellent communication skills which she exercises when talking to an individual or groups. Case in point is when she spoke in my daughter's wedding bridal shower for hours until those around kept yearning for more. I would also like to affirm that she is a God fearing woman who exhibits godly virtues and is an indispensable asset in this century we live in. We need such women in this era and age. I humbly and highly recommend her work. -M. H.

One Last Thing

Did you enjoy this book? If did and found it useful, I would be very grateful if you would take a quick 2 minutes to write a review Amazon. Your support really does make a difference as other readers will find this book. This feedback will make this book even better.

If someone you care about is struggling with the shame, stigma, guilt and pain of betrayal, please send him or her a copy of this book. If you'd like to order copies of this book for your company, school, or group of friends drop an email here sales(at)analeenie.com

If you would like to get free bonus materials from this book and receive updates on my future projects you can sign up for the newsletter NOW here eepurl.com/dLEG6Y. By signing up to the newsletter, you will great FREE access to become part of the Dream It, Pen It team and be the first to receive the next book before anyone else (even the publisher).

One Last Thing

You can also follow me on Tumblr (at)askaleen, or Pinterest (at)analeenie or analeenie.com for speaking engagements, interviews or counseling session.

Thanks again for your support.

Coming Soon

I really hope you enjoyed reading this book,

Every book that Ana writes is easy to read and direct. Future books, and especially those in the Betrayal Series solve a problem including bringing up healthy children, toxicity, relationships, healing, increasing self-esteem and self-confidence

Want to know more?

Buy Your Copy and gift love ones of the EBook and Paperback from Amazon.

Upcoming releases:

- Insecurity

- Toxicity

- Wordless Emotional Abuse

- Communication: Ways to Improve

Currently working on:

- Anger Management

- The Counselling Process

- Identity Crisis: Personal Attributes and Social Comparison

Follow the following link for other books on my Amazon Author Page:

amazon.com/author/analeen-millennialcounselor